P9-BZJ-577

NO WAY!

STRANGE FOODS

Michael J. Rosen

and Ben Kassoy

Illustrations by Doug Jones

Millbrook Press • Minneapolis

Text copyright © 2014 by Michael J. Rosen
Illustrations copyright © 2014 by Lerner Publishing Group, Inc.

All rights reserved. International copyright secured. No part of this book may be reproduced, stored in a retrieval system, or transmitted in any form or by any means—electronic, mechanical, photocopying, recording, or otherwise—without the prior written permission of Lerner Publishing Group, Inc., except for the inclusion of brief quotations in an acknowledged review.

Millbrook Press
A division of Lerner Publishing Group, Inc.
241 First Avenue North
Minneapolis, MN 55401 U.S.A.

Website address: www.lernerbooks.com

Main body text set in Adrianna Regular 12/16
Typeface provided by Chank

Rosen, Michael J.
    Strange foods / by Michael J. Rosen and Ben Kassoy ; illustrated by Doug Jones.
       p.   cm. — (No way!)
    Includes index.
    ISBN 978-0-7613-8984-2 (lib. bdg. : alk. paper)
    ISBN 978-1-4677-1707-6 (eBook)
    1. Food habits—Juvenile literature. 2. Food preferences—Juvenile literature. I. Jones, Doug, illustrator. II. Title.
    GT2850.R66 2014
    394.1'2—dc23   2012037329

Manufactured in the United States of America
1 – BP – 7/15/13

The authors would like to recognize the generous contribution of Christoffer Strömstedt, as well as the efforts of Ashley Heestand, Colin Stoecker, and Claire Hamilton in the researching, fact-checking, and drafting of the No Way! series of books.

The images in this book are used with the permission of: © Xiaofei Wang/Bon Appetit/Alamy, p. 4; © Louise Heusinkveld/Oxford Scientific/Getty Images, p. 5; © David McLain/Aurora/Getty Images, p. 7; © Ppp2010ha/Dreamstime.com, p. 8; © Neil Setchfield/Yuckfood.com/Alamy, p. 9; © Michael Freeman/Alamy, p. 11; © Neil Setchfield/Alamy, p. 13 (top); © Paul Chesley/National Geographic/Getty Images, p. 13 (bottom); Shaddack/Wikimedia Commons, p. 14; © David Greedy/Lonely Planet Images/Getty Images, p. 16; © iStockphoto.com/Sze Fei Wong, p. 17; © Jerome Whittingham/Shutterstock.com, p. 18; © Kai-Uwe Och/Colouria Media/Alamy, p. 19; AP Photo/Manish Swarup, p. 21 (top); © Bonchan/Shutterstock.com, p. 21 (bottom); AP Photo/Bullit Marquez, p. 22; © Don MacKinnon/Stringer/Getty Images, p. 23; © Karl Johaentges/LOOK/Getty Images, p. 25 (top); © Vicki Beaver/Alamy, p. 25 (bottom); © Peter Menzel/Photo Researchers, Inc., p. 26; © jigkofoto/Shutterstock.com, p. 27; © Photoshot/Hulton Archive/Getty Images, p. 29. Front cover: © Foodcollection/Getty Images.

TABLE of CONTENTS

FOR THE BiRDS
BiRD'S NEST SOUP

Maybe you eat birds—no, not sparrows or eagles but chicken tenders or turkey drumsticks. But would you ever think of snacking on a bird's *nest?*

More than fifteen hundred years ago, people in China started doing just that. They began making soup out of the nests. You might be relieved to learn that the soup does not include twigs or feathers. But then, a main ingredient in this unusual dish is saliva. Yep—spit! A bird called the Chinese swiftlet uses this sticky liquid to assemble its nest. That's right: bird-spit soup might be a more accurate name for this food.

How much would you pay for a helping of bird's nest soup? In the United States, it goes for about $100 a bowl. Why so pricey? Just ask the people who gather the nests. They climb bamboo poles to reach into high cracks in the coastal caves where swiftlets roost. Plus, the soup is said to have amazing powers. True believers who *fork* over cash to *spoon* up the soup claim that it: Boosts your immune system! Improves your complexion! Cures asthma! Slows the aging process!

Soup isn't the only place you'll find swiftlet saliva. The goo is also used to make a popular sweet. It's packed in a frilly box like Valentine's Day chocolates. Young people in China give it as gifts. Apparently, nothing says, "I love you, Mom," like a little bird drool.

Chinese swiflet nests are sometimes called white gold. At more than $2,000 a pound, (0.5 kg), it's no wonder!

DOUBLE DAIRY YOU
CASU MARZU

What's the one cheese you should wear protective goggles when eating? *Casu marzu*. It's a sheep's milk cheese from the island of Sardinia. Its tastes like ammonia. It smells like a stink bomb. But even worse, casu marzu is crawling with maggots.

That's right! This cheese is infested with little slimy wormlike creatures. These pests are known best for eating corpses. (Maybe all the good jobs were taken.) But apparently, this cheese is even *more* delicious than the dead!

This cheese from Sardinia contains no sardines, even if there *is* something awfully fishy about it!

The maggots get into casu marzu when a cheese fly (what else would this insect be named?) lays its eggs in the cheese. Limbless, clawless maggots hatch from the eggs. They use their teeth to rock climb through their curdled quarters. Shimmying along, eating, they turn the cheese into a gummy glob.

Thinking of serving a casu marzu cheese ball at your next birthday party? First, hand out those protective goggles. Cheese fly maggots can leap 6 inches (15 centimeters) in the air. Just picture the cheese as a circus tent shooting maggots instead of human cannonballs. Second, remind guests not to eat the live maggots. Why? Because they can cause some serious belly trouble in humans. So seal that cheese in a paper bag before eating it. That suffocates the maggots. Then everyone can pluck off the little buggers and simply enjoy the stinky, nauseating cheese itself.

DEVIL'S FOOD (CAKE NOT iNCLUDED)
THOUSAND-YEAR EGGS

Preserved duck and chicken eggs have been a delicacy in many Asian cultures for centuries.

Mash some mayo with a hard-boiled egg. What have you got? Deviled eggs.

Bury an egg in ashes and salt. Let it sit around for weeks. What have you got? Hmmm. What the devil eats for breakfast? It's true that the whites turn the color of Frankenstein's monster and taste like vinegar jelly. The yolks brown and smell like gas, garlic, and skunk—like the stink that's supposed to fill the air Down There. But no, this isn't the devil's breakfast. Believe it or not, it's actually a delicacy. It's also a way to preserve a bounty of eggs.

The dish is called thousand-year eggs. It comes from Asia. Want to make it? First, gather the following ingredients:

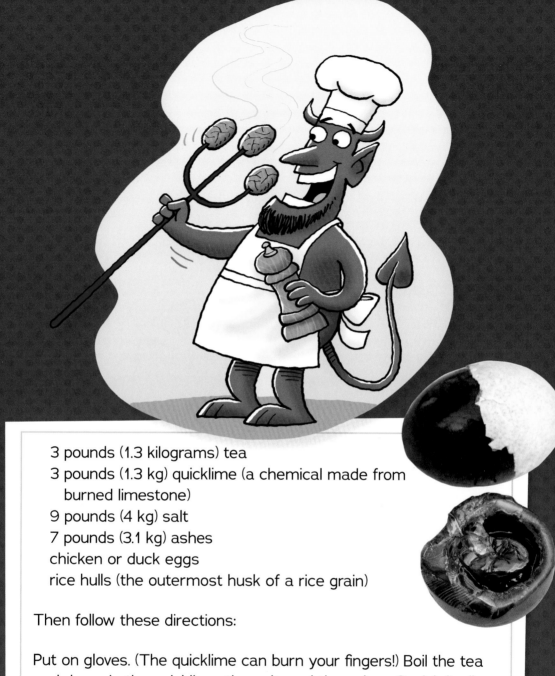

3 pounds (1.3 kilograms) tea
3 pounds (1.3 kg) quicklime (a chemical made from
    burned limestone)
9 pounds (4 kg) salt
7 pounds (3.1 kg) ashes
chicken or duck eggs
rice hulls (the outermost husk of a rice grain)

Then follow these directions:

Put on gloves. (The quicklime can burn your fingers!) Boil the tea and dump in the quicklime, the salt, and the ashes. Squish it all together to make a paste, and smear the paste around each egg. Next, roll the coated eggs in rice hulls so they won't stick to one another. Finally, shove the eggs into a covered container. Ignore them. (No, really. Don't even say hello to them for several weeks.) After that, take out the eggs and crack open the crusty shell that's hardened around them. Put a clothespin on your nose. Then eat up! *Nom nom nom.* Makes you wonder what the devil eats for lunch.

YAKKING iT UP
YAK BUTTER TEA

Imagine this: You're bundled in clothing and blankets woven of yak hair. You're warming yourself by a fire that burns yak dung. So what are you drinking? Yak butter tea, of course!

For the nomadic people of the Himalayan regions (an area in southern Asia), that's a pretty common scene. The hairy, horned yak is important to them. It's their form of transportation. It's their source of fuel. It's also their food. Tibetans cook yak meat, sure. But they also make butter, yogurt, and cheese from yak milk—it's *udderly* delicious!

The butter (as you probably guessed) is a key ingredient in yak butter tea. This tea supplies a majority of a person's fluids and calories in the Himalayas. Plus, the buttery fat acts like lip balm!

The national beverage of Tibet, this tea is thick, salty, smoky, bitter, yellow-brown, and greasy. (Hmm. Which of those qualities keeps the tea from really catching on around the globe? How about *all of them!*) To keep warm in their chilly climate, nomadic Tibetan people drink more than forty cups a day. They are pretty small cups—but still, that's quite a bit of tea.

Ready to brew a little yak butter tea? First, boil a special kind of smoky, bitter tea leaf. Next, pour the tea into a churn. Add some yak butter and salt. Beat until it's foamy. Then, yakety-yak, toss it down the hatch!

People in Tibet love yak butter tea. Maybe they'd think root beer, lemonade, or cocoa was disgusting!

Other Bizarre Brews around the Globe

- Yogurt Pepsi (carbonated sour milk) from Japan

- Baby mouse wine (dead baby mice soaked in rice wine) from China

- Seagull wine (a dead seagull soaked in water and left to warm in the sun) from Alaska

- Bovine urine (cow pee) from India

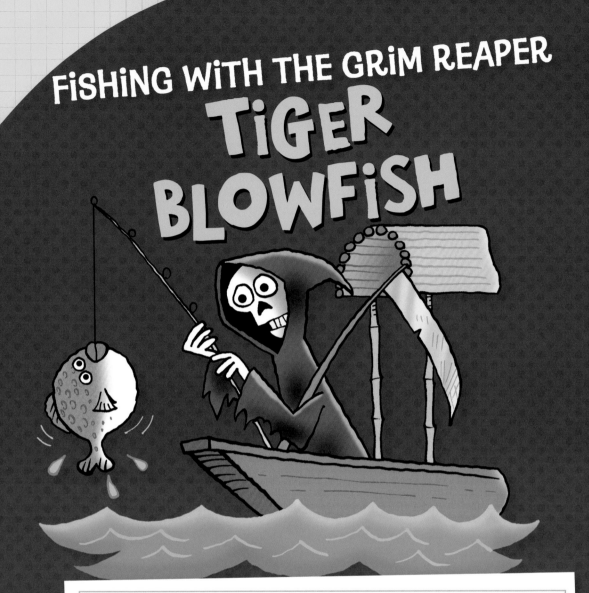

FISHING WITH THE GRIM REAPER
TIGER BLOWFISH

Blowfish are bottom-feeding creatures that can inflate their bodies into spiny balls. They are also a tasty treat to adventurous seafood lovers. There are more than three hundred species of blowfish. One of them—called the tiger fugu—is considered the filet mignon of blowfish. It's the choice cut—if your choice is distinctive flavor combined with deadly poison, that is.

Blowfish are highly toxic. Their poison, called tetrodotoxin, is so potent that the amount needed to kill a sumo wrestler fits on the head of a pin. And the cure? There isn't one.

Only specially licensed chefs may prepare tiger fugu. The law even requires these chefs to keep the discarded bits of fish under lock and key! Otherwise, Dumpster divers could be diving to their deaths.

Why do people take chances and eat this potentially deadly fish? Blowfish lovers say that the flesh has a divine, delicate freshness. They say that the itty-bitty amount of poison they eat when they munch on the fish creates a lovely, numbing sensation on the lips and tongue. *Numb . . . Yum!*

What they don't say (and probably don't even want to think about) is what happens if you eat just the teensiest bit too much. First, dizziness, exhaustion, and nausea set in. Then the muscles freeze up—including the lips and tongue; the arms and legs; and, eventually, the heart and lungs. Is a bite of tasty fish worth the chance of dying? More and more people say yes. The dish used to be eaten mostly in Japan. But these days, diners can play Go Fish with the Grim Reaper in Philadelphia, Chicago, and Los Angeles.

Ready to take a bite out of this blowfish? Well, maybe not.

MORE TRICK THAN TREAT

PECULIAR CANDIES

Is your idea of candy a sugary burst of fruit? A crispy, chocolaty chunk? Or how about one of these international treats?

Salmiakki

If pirates ate licorice, *salmiakki* would be their fav. This candy is as black as a crow, as hard as asphalt, and as salty as the sea itself. In Denmark, Finland, and Norway, this tarlike salt-lick rules. Some varieties even contain ammonium chloride. That's table salt bonded with ammonia, which gives this candy a fishy taste.

Echizen Kurage

What is *echizen kurage*? It's a 6-foot (1.8-meter), 440-pound (199 kg) jellyfish. Run away! Or you could blend it with burnt

14

sugar to create a fish-flavored caramel. Or try another Japanese treat: chocolate-covered dried squid. Or grilled-lamb caramels. Makes you wonder if candy-coated prune pits or erasers are on the dessert menu as well.

Musk Candy

An animal called the musk deer lives in the mountains of Asia. The male has a gland that makes musk, a substance with a really strong odor. It smells earthy, woodsy, and "beasty." It's used to attract mates. Funnily, humans find the scent attractive too. Small amounts of musk are used in making perfumes!

Does this scream "candy" to you? It does to people in Australia and New Zealand. In those countries, folks with a sweet tooth can enjoy musk lollipops, musk Lifesavers, musk gum, and other things that sound like a big mistake . . . or should we say *musk*-take?

THE ONLY FRUIT YOU HARVEST IN A HARD HAT
DURIAN

The unusual, prickly durian fruit is native to some parts of Asia.

Durian is sometimes called the king of fruits. So is it the biggest fruit? The tastiest? The most popular? Nope. Durian gets called king because it is the *baddest!*

Durian is stinky, thorny, and almost impossible to open. Outside, it's a greenish-yellow porcupine—a thick, 1-foot-long (0.3 m) husk with spikes. Indeed, if this "king" falls on *your* crown, it can cause serious wounds.

Inside . . . well, the oozing center of this funky fruit reeks! People can't exactly describe the durian's smell. Rotten onions, turpentine, and gym socks are some suggestions that have been thrown out. The durian has such a stench that it's been banned from public transportation and hotels in many areas. That's right: the king has been exiled!

While durians make humans run for cover, the fruit's fumes actually attract animals from up to 1 mile (1.6 kilometers) away! So, if your dog is ever lost, put a durian on your doorstep. Sparky may come running home . . . along with pigs, elephants, and even tigers. That's because many animals love to eat the durian.

And indeed, if you can get past the smell, durian pulp is delicious—to people as well as animals. Again, people can't describe the taste. Some say it's like cream cheese or butterscotch. With such a tasty, unusual flavor, it's no surprise that this fruit gives the "royal treatment" to everything from custard and candy to coffee drinks and fish soups.

FOUL FISH, FISHY FOWL
SURSTRÖMMING, HONGEO, AND KIVIAK

You've probably eaten fermented foods. Bread, yogurt, pickles—these are all fermented, or chemically changed by exposure to bacteria over time. But just because you might enjoy these treats doesn't mean you'll like everything that's been fermented. Take the following foods, for example.

Surströmming
Swedes spend an eternity preparing their fermented fish dish called *surströmming*. From pickling the fish to packing it in cans,

the process takes over a year. The result? A dish that seems to be composed of rotten eggs, rancid butter, and farts. In fact, the pressure and gas that builds during the fermentation of surströmming can be explosive! Many airlines have even banned it. Ready to dig in? Yeah, didn't think so.

Hongeo

Koreans serve a raw, dreadful sea creature called a skate—a kind of ray with fins that act like underwater wings. When it's prepared, it's called *hongeo*. If the words *raw* and *skate* didn't make you gag, this will: pee. Yep, that, too, is an ingredient in hongeo. See, skates don't have bladders, so their pee comes out through their skin. When hongeo is prepared, that pee turns to ammonia. It's like dipping a forkful of fish in window-cleaning fluid.

Kiviak

This delicacy comes from Greenland. To make it, cooks stuff hundreds of auks—a web-footed diving bird—inside a gutted seal. Then the seal's skin is sewn shut and greased. Months later, usually at a wedding or other celebration, the birds are unpacked. The heads are snapped off, and the fermented juice inside is sucked down. Party on!

BHUT JOLOKIA CHiLi

"It's so hot you can't even imagine," one farmer says about the *bhut jolokia*. "When you eat it, it's like dying."

This scorching veggie from India is one of Earth's hottest chilis. You know how earthquakes are rated on the Richter scale? Well, Scoville Heat Units (SHU) are what's used for measuring spiciness. Jalapeño peppers score between 2,500 and 5,000 SHU. The bhut jolokia, by comparison, scores over one million. At more than four hundred times spicier than most hot sauces, it makes your average chili seem . . . well, kind of chilly!

Bhut jolokia is almost like pepper spray. In fact, Indian police do sometimes use this chili in sprays to break up riots. It's also found in smoke bombs that force terrorists or criminals out of hiding. As they say, if you can't take the heat, get out of the kitchen . . . or that underground bunker.

Even elephants aren't a match for the bhut jolokia. Farmers smear chili powder on their fences to keep pesky pachyderms off the premises—permanently. As they say, an elephant never forgets.

Aside from countering terrorism and elephants, the pepper is used in sauces and pastes, although even a single bite can make your eyes water and your nose run. That may sound unpleasant, but the pepper supposedly has healing powers. Some claim it can cure stomachaches. Others recommend eating it to actually cool the body during summer (if you can take the heat, that is).

These peppers are so flaming hot that you might have to call the fire department to put out your burning taste buds!

CUP O' KITTY POO
KOPI LUWAK

Some morning, to really warm your father's heart, fill his World's Greatest Dad mug with coffee made from poop (seriously!). But save up: that one cup will run you thirty bucks (no, *seriously!*).

Kopi luwak is the world's costliest coffee. And, yes, it's brewed from poop—poop from an animal called the Asian palm civet, to be exact. This creature is a marsupial, like opossums and kangaroos. It's also often known as a toddy cat—although *potty* cat might be a better name for it!

How does cat poop end up in coffee? Well, toddy cats eat the berry of the coffee tree. Inside the berries are coffee beans. When toddy cats eat the berries, they also swallow the beans.

This guy's doo-doo makes one pricey cup of coffee.

22

The beans pass through the animal's digestive system, where chemicals called enzymes soak into the beans. Then the toddy cat poops them out. People swear that the enzymes give the beans a special flavor.

Just how—or why—someone first decided to gather toddy cat poop and brew it remains a mystery. But those who love the coffee aren't complaining. They say kopi luwak coffee is smooth, mellow, and—now try not to think too much about poop here—*chocolatey.* They gladly put their money where their mouth is for a taste of this unusual drink. And at ten or twenty times the price of other coffee, kopi luwak *must be* good to the last dropping!

FEETING FRENZY
EDIBLE FEET

Toe jam. Blisters. Odor. Lots of people won't even go near feet, let alone put them in their mouth. But eatin' feet is a big part of many cuisines. You could say the world's in a *feet*ing frenzy!

In South Africa, chicken feet are boiled up and chomped down. Served alone, they're known as "runaways." Order them with a chicken head, and you've got what they call a "walkie talkie." (No kidding—they really do call them that. But admittedly, that bird isn't doing much of either.)

Grilled chicken feet with vegetables is party food in Jamaica. Mix yams, bananas, dumplings, scallions, and peppers in a broth with chicken feet, and you've got chicken-foot soup.

In China, chicken feet are a snack food. Prepackaged and often vinegar-flavored, they're sold alongside peanuts and chips. Next time you're in a checkout line in China, plead with Mom to buy you chicken feet instead of a box of mints or gum.

Over in Norway, pig's hooves are preferred to chicken feet. They're a traditional Christmas dish there. Boiled and salt-cured, the hooves are served as finger food. (No word on whether Santa prefers pig's hooves to cookies and milk.) People in Japan seem to love the rich flavor of pig's hooves too. They're put in everything from stews to dumplings.

Are you up for chowing down on feet? They're nutritious! Hooves contain collagen, a protein that keeps skin moist and makes hair shiny. So go ahead and *pig* out!

WAITER! THERE'S A BUG ON MY PLATE!
GIANT WATER BUG SAUCE

If a 4-inch-long (10 cm) bug suddenly trotted across your dinner plate, you'd probably scream, "Yuck!" But if you lived in Vietnam, you might say, "Yum!" Bugs are popular foods there—and in many other nations, where more than one thousand species of bugs are eaten regularly.

The giant water bug *Lethocerus indicus* is a favorite in Vietnam. It's longer than your hand is wide. It's mostly used to make a popular food flavoring. Male *Lethocerus indicus* produce a liquid that's used to make the flavoring. It can take a few hundred bugs just to make a single spoonful! Good thing that one drop is all that's needed to flavor a bowl of soup.

In addition to soup, the flavoring is used on noodles and in sauces. The Vietnamese think it adds a little something extra to these dishes. They might pour it on food the way you'd add salt or hot sauce.

So what's the flavoring taste like? It's a little fishy, like scallops or shrimp. It gives foods a salty and somewhat meaty flavor.

Ready to add some creepy crawlies to your diet? Just remember the bug eater's golden rule: "If it moves, it's bad news. But if it's fried, give it a try!"

GIANT WATER BUG SAUCE

A DISH TO DIE FOR
EATING POISON

Long ago, the enemies of King Mithridates—a ruler who once controlled Turkey—served him a poisoned dinner. He scarfed it down. And lived to tell about it. How?

Mithridates suspected his enemies might poison him. So for years, he ate teensy tidbits of poison. He built up his body's immunity to it so the meal that should have killed him merely filled him.

Even in modern times, people sometimes consume poison. The practice is called mithridatism. It's done to encourage the body to produce more of the substances it needs to protect itself from poison.

Bill Haast practiced mithridatism. This serpentologist (snake expert) ate venom for twenty-five years. And it saved him! He was bitten

Serpentologist Bill Haast made snake venom a regular part of his diet.

by snakes more than one hundred times, but because he was completely used to venom, he survived to the age of one hundred.

Others practice mithridatism by eating—get this—*poison ivy!* That's right: They don't want poison ivy *on* their bodies, so they put it *in* their bodies! They use a slice of bread to grasp a leaf from a stem. They swallow the bread without touching their lips. They say repeating this process makes their bodies used to the poison so they don't break out when they do touch this itch-inducing plant. (Warning: do not try this the next time you're out in the woods. Eating plants in the woods can be extremely dangerous!)

Venom and poison ivy are gross enough, but what's even grosser? Some people drink their own pee! They often mix it with nutritional drinks and drink it in the morning. They claim that this "urine therapy" boosts their health in many ways. Sounds like a good reason to skip breakfast.

GLOSSARY

ammonia: a colorless, sharp-smelling gas

ammonium chloride: table salt bonded with ammonia

carbonated: combined or filled with the gas carbon dioxide. Some beverages are carbonated to give them bubbles.

collagen: a protein that keeps skin moist and makes hair shiny. Animal hooves are one source of collagen.

delicacy: a food that is considered special or luxurious

enzyme: any one of various proteins in humans and animals that bring about or speed up certain processes, such as digestion

fermented: chemically changed by exposure to bacteria

immune system: the bodily system that protects people from illnesses

maggot: a slimy, wormlike creature that grows into a flying insect

marsupial: a type of animal including opossums, kangaroos, wombats, and toddy cats. Female marsupials usually have a pouch for carrying their young.

mithridatism: the practice of eating small amounts of poison so the body becomes used to it

musk: a substance made by the male musk deer. Musk has an earthy, woodsy scent.

nomadic: roaming from place to place

pachyderm: any of various animals that have thick skin and hooves or nails that resemble hooves. Elephants, rhinoceroses, and hippopotamuses are pachyderms.

rancid: having a strong, disagreeable smell or taste

saliva: a mixture of water, antibacterial agents, and enzymes found in the mouths of animals (including humans). Saliva is sometimes known as spit.

Scoville Heat Units (SHU): a unit used for measuring spiciness in food

suffocate: to stop the breathing of a living thing

toxic: poisonous

SOURCE NOTE

Tim Sullivan, "When You Eat It, It's Like Dying," *Brisbane Times,* August 1, 2007, http://www.brisbanetimes.com.au/articles/2007/08/01/1185647946289.html (August 29, 2012).

FURTHER READING

BOOKS

Higgins, Nadia. *Fun Food Inventions.* Minneapolis: Lerner Publications Company, 2014.
Get the inside scoop on all kinds of fun treats that kids love to eat—no bugs or rotten eggs included!

King, Bart. *The Big Book of Gross Stuff.* Layton, UT: Gibbs Smith, 2010.
Can't get enough of all things gross? Then you'll love this book that covers everything from burping and sneezing to stinky cheese.

Rosenberg, Pam. *Eek! Icky, Sticky, Gross Stuff in Your Food.* Mankato, MN: Child's World, 2008.
In this fun and breezy—yet disgusting!—read, you'll learn about fried grasshoppers, duck's blood soup, and many other "delicacies" enjoyed around the world.

WEBSITES

GROSSOLOGY: THE SCIENCE OF REALLY GROSS THINGS
http://www.grossology.org
This website includes all kinds of hilarious gross stuff for you to read about and do. You can even find recipes for blood soup and dookie cookies. Yum-yum.

MYPLATE: HEALTH AND NUTRITION INFORMATION FOR CHILDREN
http://www.choosemyplate.gov/children-over-five.html
Want to find out what you *should* be eating? (Hint: It's not toxic fish or chicken feet.) Then head over to the United States Department of Agriculture's website about healthful eating.

INDEX

For Mike

Text and Illustrations copyright © 2006 by Jeff Newman • All rights reserved.

Little, Brown and Company • Time Warner Book Group • 1271 Avenue of the Americas, New York, NY 10020
Visit our Web site at www.lb-kids.com

Library of Congress Cataloging-in-Publication Data

Newman, Jeff.
Hippo! No, rhino / by Jeff Newman.—1st ed.
p. cm.
Summary: When a careless worker places the wrong sign near a rhinoceros's cage, zoo visitors continually mistake
the frustrated rhino for a hippopotamus, until a young boy comes along who can help.
ISBN 0-316-15573-X
[1. Rhinoceroses—Fiction. 2. Mistaken identity—Fiction. 3. Zoos—Fiction.] I. Title.
PZ7.N47984Hi 2006
[E]—dc22
2004042327

First Edition: July 2006   10 9 8 7 6 5 4 3 2 1   TWP   Printed in Singapore.

The illustrations for this book were done in pencil, ink, marker, watercolor, gouache, colored pencil,
pastel, and cut paper on 150 lb. Cold Press Fabriano Artistico watercolor paper.

The text was set in Garamond and hand-lettered by Jeff Newman, and the display type was set in
WakWacOops!, ZemkeHand, and hand-lettered by Jeff Newman.

JORDAN
PZ7
.N47984
Hi
2006

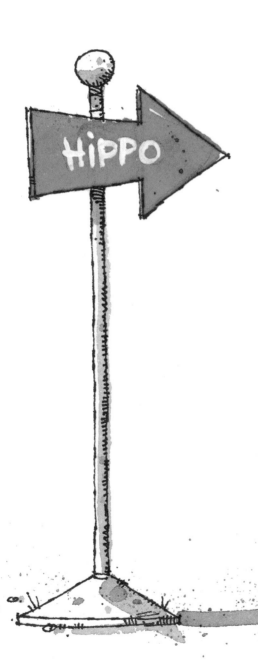

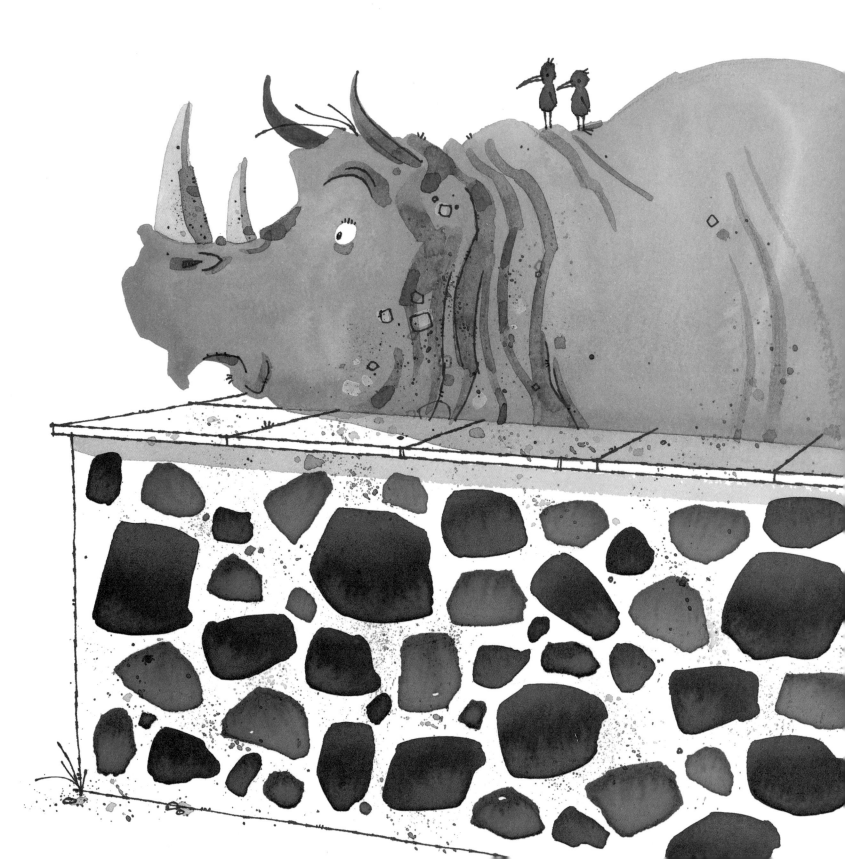

THAT'S NOT

MINE-O!

HIPPO

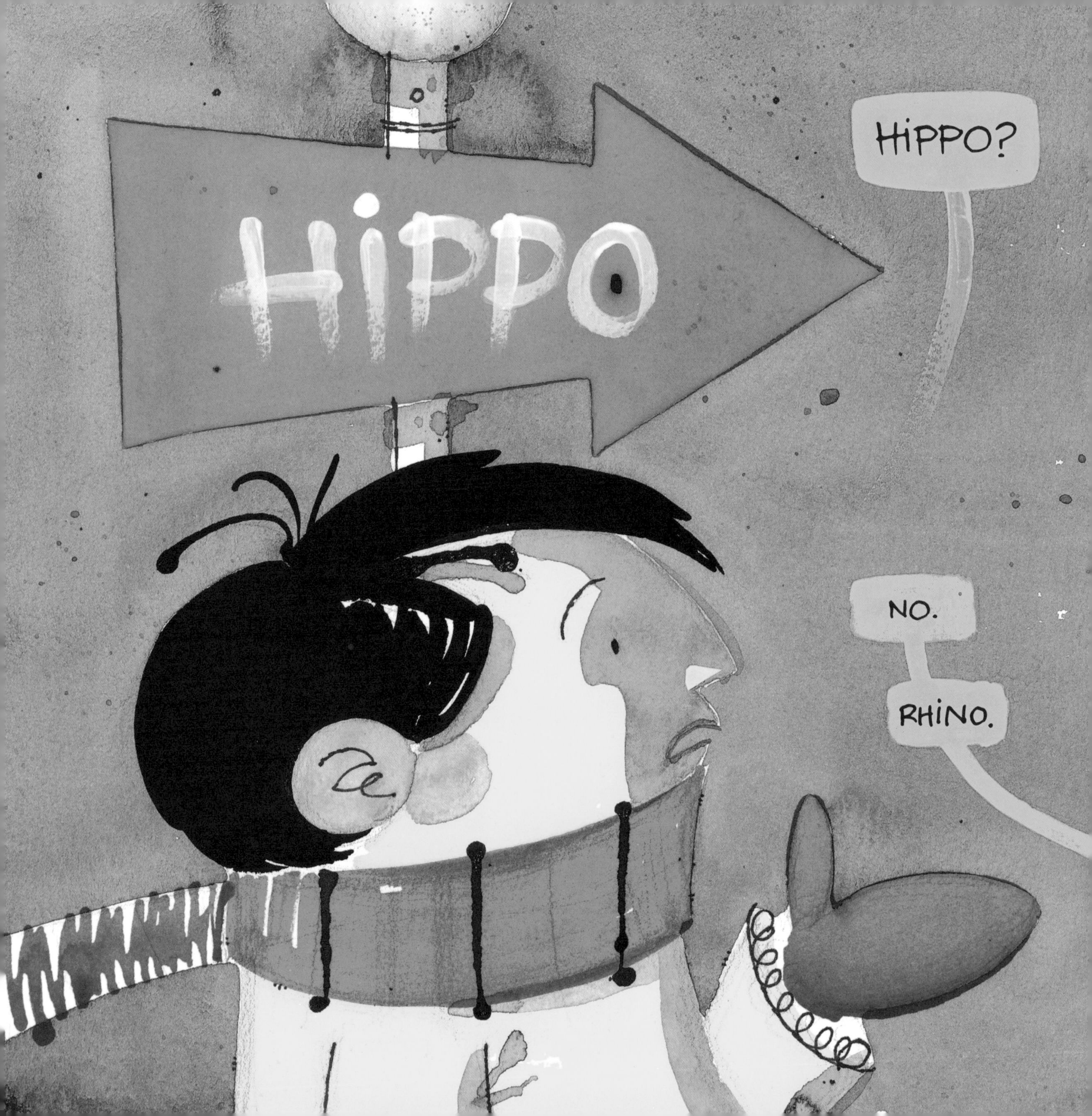
HIPPO
HIPPO?
NO.
RHINO.

BOSTON PUBLIC LIBRARY

3 9999 05097 880 6

Allston Branch Library
300 N. Harvard Street
Allston, MA 02134